THE HOUSE THAT HOLDS

to lisa —
with admiration!
& affection

The House That Holds

POEMS

Love,

Buff Lindau

Buff

ONION
RIVER
PRESS

Burlington, Vermont

ISBN: 978-1-949066-65-4

Onion River Press
191 Bank Street
Burlington, VT 05401

for Huck
and Ben and Dave
and Max
and Jenny and Lena

Contents

Poems from Our Climate   **99**

Praise

The House that Holds

Tiger and whale, bear and squirrel—
shapes of the cakes for two boys
who graced the house with purpose
from birth to day care to school days
with backpacks, boots, and sticky good-byes.

Their baseballs, gloves and things
still piled in closets and garage,
skis, a clutter in the basement,
caps and gowns, high chair and rocking horse,
all bunked in with the washer and dryer.

A city dwelling with roses and peonies,
neighbors, cats, storms and us, long married,
lodged in the house. Its quirks and ours
etched deep in the walls, floors, synapses,
well known each to each.

Kitchen, bedroom, garden, all witness
to the twists of family life—
eruptions, embraces, tears and applause—
right down to the creak of the stairs,
the turn of our selves in the night.

The intimacy of laundry—his socks,
matched and rolled a hundred times,
weekend cappuccino, slow

round the kitchen table
of oranges, muffins, music.

Through slammed doors, faulty plumbing,
creaky storm windows jimmied into place
to contain our weathers, the house embraces
our ways, our clutter of books, CDs,
paintings, pottery, aches and pains and wrinkles.

Our rhythms and sighs, turnings and couplings
rocked into sleep in nightly refuge, nightly wonder
through to morning's waltz around and between—
synchronized rhythms of breakfast, dinners, gardens, moments—
as we dwell a while longer in this house that holds us.

We have an encounter
sometimes in the garden

(for my mother)

I see her shake topsoil from each weed
to give to favored plantings

that she coddled into bloom the way she hoped
she could shake missteps from us four,

make us flourish, grow right out of the house—
and away.

Half a century later I shake each weed the same,
a legacy in tribute to her gardening skills.

I hold tight in refusal, won't let her slip away,
though years, visions, memories vanish bit by bit, on and on.

*　*　*

She grew a great blooming bushy garden without help.
She escaped into a world of trees and shrubs and flowering things—

daisies, verbena, pansies flourished along her borders and paths.
Rows of bright red anemones marched straight up to the front door.

She dressed our white brick corner house

in azaleas camellias dogwood magnolia

daffodils, a grape arbor, a fig tree wrapped in gauze
to keep birds from the lush fruits—which she fed to us, her greedy
    young.

*　*　*

She kneels and digs and walks with me
as I toss weeds in a pile or bucket or
quick in a bush, as she sometimes did.

We take the garden cure, the garden refuge.
Her shape, her face, her habit of stealth retreat
follow me from garden patch to garden patch—

you'd think she had a bottle hid, but never did.

*　*　*

My wisteria won't bloom, but it conjures hers,
hung heavy with fragrant purple clusters,

perfuming weekend spring breakfasts
of popovers, biscuits, flakey pastry.

With these visions comes a plague of her worries
proffered by all four of us—

my wrong-headed romances and the other three.
Would one daughter ever marry?
Would the only son divorce? Would the bookend two
take care of the middle two?

*　*　*

In the garden she was free, unburdened,

moving quietly above family heartache.

Gone these thirty years, that's how I'll fix her.
I'll take a lesson for my own journey,

and find her above the fears, floating, beautiful,
deep in the roses, grape vines and glorious floribundas.

Okay, So the Red Sox Let Us Down, 9-29-11

if the Red Sox had to have another
catastrophic, historic, unsightly collapse,
at least this time our boys
watched the unspeakable outcome together
traveled by train from DC
to Camden Yards to what became
the total demise
of this once robust sure-thing season

over which I too am disappointed
along with all fans and relatives of fans
of the quixotic Sox

but there's huge compensating comfort
that our sons, ten years apart in age
are living now in the same locale
are on the same wave length
and hang out together—
and charged up after work
went, brothers, to what would be the Sox debacle

I think especially of the jokes they have
one makes and the other laughs
and the history, the parents—
our foibles and tentacles

so the Red Sox disappoint
I wish they were winners for us all
but the boys, oh boy,
the boys watched it in the bleachers
with beer and hot dogs together
now and forward into the future

taste

there was a page
in a picture book
that Ben always licked--
every time we sat
sidled up close for reading
it was just too delicious to resist

over and over and over
its coming was no surprise--
still, excitement mounted
he got ready, eyes wide, breath held
as it crept closer page by page

there it was again
and he had to taste it
no fuss, just his tongue on the page
of the pinky purpley sea anemone
floating in Swimmy's underwater world
back when Ben was small
and I was certain

now he's swimming in his own world
afloat in scopes and scales and fancy things--
might as well be under water--
discovering the microbes in cells

the crinkly page in the much-licked Swimmy

calls forth five-year-old Ben
along with grown-up Ben
now miles away
still wide-eyed exploring
tasting the taste of worlds
forever unknown to me

The Catastrophe Gene

Face to face with a bear in Alaska--
I wonder just how close
my son came to catastrophe
when his boss spit out the words,
'Get in the truck.'

Unscathed but uncorrected
by that singular encounter,
how could he not walk headlong
into the family hegemony,

the paternal bent, not to say lament
towards danger, radiating out
now for generations of
sublimations and inclinations.

One night his dad mis-stepped off
a Himalayan cliff edge in Assam
to land on a ledge where he lodged
till shouts drew a monk's rescue.

His encounter with a power tool
turned from catastrophe to romance,
marriage, and this very son,
bequeathed with the family predisposition.

Further back the son's father's father

started it with a mystery hospital bout
steeped in burdens and ambitions,
coursing along an immigrant's route.
No wonder we had to rock
this one up and down the street
through the hard colic of babyhood,
sing him out of wakeful nights,

watch him race his heart out
on ski slopes across the Green Mountains,
where he trained for the joyous misery
of a split-second missed slalom gate.

Now his gene-linked midnight calls
strike us wide-eyed again
absorbing the scenario—bears, cliffs, hospitals—
this time a missed train:

a continent and ocean distant.
They de-coupled the baggage car
where he napped while his friends rumbled on
to Oktoberfest.

Lead player, center stage,
rarely missing from a scene
in the episodes that stoke our drama.

His latest misadventure
a skiing fling, quick turns,
fast carves, slalom gates,
the inevitable crashing end.

The right hand of a would-be chef broken.
Now it's casted, along with the die

and him out West on his own.

The family heritage, the litany of the risky gene—
albatross for a son drawn to locales of danger,
yet a lynx, quick beautiful intent, moving on,
and us lying wide awake, watching.

Orion's Hill

Wide spread arms stretch forth
to claim the empyrean,
stalwart legs stand firm
lording over our speck of Earth.

His brilliant three-star belt,
the shining dagger thrusting
deep into the air we breathe
on a clear spring night

Orion rides tall, unmoved by earthly matters,
villain, lumbering, useless giant,
fraud of a presence, leering from on high
disporting his monumental self,
heaven's barbarian, clad in bright stars.

Walking up the hill, I remember
that big-hearted beautiful girl,
her face smiling from the pages
of the paper till they found her killer.
Her cell phone dead. Her judgment flawed.
Her sweetness to blame.
Picked up on this hill for her last ride.

Orion watched, cared nothing,
yet displays himself, brazen,
while the taint of murder lurks in dark patches

past the school where my two went.

Full of bravado and fake protection,
Orion's sky-filling presence
reigns mindless, an affront
to our small plight on Earth—
yet glorious, still, mammoth
amongst all the stars.

Sheesham & Lotus

My friend and I headed out
into the Vermont hills at dusk,
spring just emerging
light greeny-yellow on mountain hillsides
meadows rocks valleys and vistas
willows wafting in gold
the occasional elegant horse
on a gallop or easy loping walk –
through miles of new spring glory
into the raucous fun of old-time music.

Deep in the woods we arrived
at the Ripton Community Coffee House
filled with fans bearded and tie-dyed
in work-shirts hiking boots, flowery skirts,
ready for the homespun talents of Sheesham and Lotus
decked out in bowlers, suspenders, vests and striped pants,
one tall and handsome, one short and eccentric.
They moved us to tapping nodding clapping
to their high-stepping mountain music.
With fiddle and kazoo banjo trumpet vocals,
they offered us charm and gusto, talent and tales.
They transported us beyond the fears we always raise we two.
We friends of forty years,
we always come back and back
to the world we're leaving our children and theirs—
rising seas, poisoned air, politics of fear deceit inaction.

We fell into the transporting gift of a magical evening,
with the uncanny duo of Sheesham and Lotus
and the immense, the star-filled country night.

Bread and Puppet!

revives us every year with charm and challenge—
spread out in a natural amphitheater
way up in the Northeast Kingdom of Vermont
the unstoppable pageantry—white clad troupes
of dancers, singers, horn section and kids
all rollicking in their assigned roles
the indomitable brilliance of the pageant on rolling hills

giant winged bird puppets on long poles
with stern stories of our despoiling of the earth
and scenes applauding the glory of nature

Peter Schumann now in his eightieth year
dancing to "When the Saints"
on twenty-foot high stilts, in Uncle Sam top hat
red and white striped pants

we gathered in the silence of trees
moving with huge papier-maché potatoes before us
grouped in the pine forest in quiet assembly
as Schumann played violin and spoke poetry

next we potatoes followed en masse
to a hill topped by giant sun puppets
on long poles beside mothers of earth
the quiet enormity of it
drum tones echoing big messages

and the long drive home
steeped in the magic of circus, the pageant
the sweeping hills, pine forest
and enormous cloud-filled sky

Ella and Marilyn

(both born April 25, 1926)

Amazing to hear *A Tisket A Tasket*
by the high priestess of jazz singers.
Marilyn Monroe loved Ella too
invited her to sing at a midtown club,
sat at the front table night after night—

and so brought Ella from the Apollo to Mocambo
from Harlem to the fancy swells.
The press followed Marilyn, found Ella
and her epic voice soared round the world.

Finished to a perfect glow, Marilyn,
so lovely so exposed, so talented so young
married Joe then Arthur.
The world gaped and gawked
"Some Like it Hot," "Something's Got to Give,"
a star too big, the world too close—
blonde, thirty-six, and she was gone,
skirt blown high in the air, a pin-up forever

Ella, pearly smooth voice, ladylike, lyrical,
phrasing, range, and heart—all perfection—
sweet jazz for fifty years
unmatched still, indebted, she said,
to Marilyn who got her an upscale gig

and so she took Manhattan
held it rapt with song, high priestess forever

Marilyn—exquisite, vulnerable,
beyond glamorous, short-lived

icons, so unlikely to be linked

There's a Staircase in Urbino

steeped in Italian history and style—
peopled by elegant ladies and gents
with turn of the head, turn of the phrase
point of the toe, tilt of the shoulder just so
gloved hands on hips—
all effortless, knowing, intrinsic

only Italians could do
that marble staircase
deep inside the castle
tapestried walls all around
wide shallow steps
smoothed from centuries of wear
just right for a horse to step up
step by step
slowly ascending with easy grace
high stepping knees, nostrils wide, mane flouncing
head high, rider high
elegance beyond style—
into the heart of the ducal palace

were the ladies faint of heart
when the coal black stallion strode up the wide marble staircase
saddle bridle and stirrup gilded with gold
handsome rider astride—

his knowing nod, courtly smile
feathered hat, leg-o-mutton puffed sleeves
sleek jodhpurs
rich magenta brocade

imagine the Duke of Urbino
Federico da Montefeltro
immortal profile in paint
nose etched by gunshot
wearing a high-collared, red damask coat
now just think of the Duke on horseback
head high on both rider and horse
the click of the hooves on the marble
the waft of the tall feathered hat

Noche Flamenca in Vermont

Each one tasted her power,
the pounding beat of her heart
her soulful self, rhythmic stomps,
wild contorted dance, potent swirls
of blind romance.

Bull and matador at once—
intensity was all for Soledad.
Her passion roiled towards
unleashed aggression,
electrified the air, ruled the house.

Partners encircled, encroached
urged her in song, percussive claps,
noble guitars, syncopated heels
tapping rat-a-tatting,
full-throated escalating song.

She lured out a partner
himself a wonder to behold—
tight pants high-heeled boots
devotion—then she threw him back,
danced alone, deep in another zone.

Two sinuous beauties, eyes flashing,
rhythms mounting,
mere supplicants to Soledad,

reached for her orbit
as she wound herself tight,
swirling seducing exhorting.

The *Noche Flamenca* family
sang, danced and played her
onward into throbbing rivers
of lust and bite—
so Latin, so impossibly urbane.

The Family House

vibes and voices, pets and parties
the parents the secrets
the Seinfeld stories and Simpson jokes
stuff from babyhood to graduation—
earmarks and landmarks . . .

My two need to find the house
that will nurture, not smother.
Ours, a cocoon, an embrace
of art and books, jokes and stories,
a world perhaps too cozy, too something or other.
Now they circle and search for their own.

The house stands near-empty since out they went
leaving rooms bereft of boys
hollow spaces crowned with ski trophies
science medals, trucks, soccer gear
Legos and baseball cards.

A house with a cat or two each decade
gardens and menus changing year by year
through grade school and crossing guards
Little League, summer camp, SATs
the scraps and scrapes, the frolics and uproars
in the kitchen, round the dinner table
by window niche and backyard garden.

Will they find the house that holds a family
tight in a grip to nurture and define
through bar mitzvahs, barbeques, birthdays
breakfasts and dinners: pancakes, pot roast, spaghetti, grits?

Did the mix of genes and sports and picture books
make up for lapses in music lessons, foreign languages?
Does the house let go and let them out?
Or does it hover tight? Will they land their own
with gardens of peonies on a street with neighbors—
a place to raise children
a house to grow up in and go out from?

Sons and Grandson

Dave setting off

A chill in the air signals
fall's familiar start of school
and there sits Dave, eager, anxious,
gearing up for a leap into the unknown
without school or a cadre of friends
to anchor his days and nights
for the first time in his young life.

Dave about to take his degree,
leave behind the zapper, the couch,
the short-order-cooking jobs, give up
skis and soccer cleats, carousing
with college mates, and take the plunge
into grown-up city life.

Glancing in his room, I'm caught
by the vibe of someone just out of reach,
gone, but hovering still in the books,
posters, sneakers, baseball cards,
bar mitzvah scroll, college notebooks
dotted with drawings and notes,
"Will this class ever end?"

Over all looms the coming silence,
and me, missing his jokes and pokes,
his "You might be the devil" accusations,
his quick-step tap dance to the music,

while sniffing out what's for dinner.

He's educated, shod, washed and shorn,
ready to cut loose.
Can I stop imagining him losing his wallet,
credit card, cell phone? His luggage could get lost
with his first-ever new suit. He could get lost.

The other one out West held by his lab work,
sending handmade pottery home for gifts—
his blue-eyed sweetness.
And now this one's green eyes,
leaving too.

Vessels of Touch

Handsome, brainy, private,
he's well known to me, he's mine.
I watched the growing up,
the steadfast curiosity
that led to paint and plants, math and art.
But now on the phone
I can't unlock the words.
I parse each phrase, each monosyllable.
I replay and rehear words, tone, the few facts.
Was it flat, inflected, fraught?
I muddle along wondering
what was hidden there.
I imagine catastrophe,
then decide to shake off
this tiresome mothering

and embrace the known.
A runner, skier, scientist,
who likes best to shape shapes,
form vases and vessels and bowls,
ramekins, casseroles, coffee cups,
pots for oatmeal, Seder plates.
I envision his hands
throwing a ceramic shape,
forming the porcelain,
pulling and molding it just so.

These vessels of touch
on the sill above the kitchen sink
speak to me in a language
direct and eloquent, if soundless,
every time I wash a dish or peel a potato.
They grace the dining table, kitchen table, bureau—
vases, pitchers, teapots—articulate and clear.

I marvel at the celadon green, ocean blue,
hints of turquoise, swirls painted in,
lines drawn to match the shapes,
a mountain range etched around.
I handle the forms, their smoothness
a connection to his hands at work—
his words captured in clay,
bodied forth whole.

Soil Knife

My artist son so deft shaping clay
into beautiful cups and vessels and bowls,
so calming with his two-year-old son—
whose garbled rendition of LMNOP, by-the-way,
is downright epic—sent this surprise gift, a soil knife.

On my birthday, two gifts, his son's ABCs recorded
and the soil knife—mysterious, ominous,
while the grandson's voice spoke wonderful and true!
But who needs to knife the soil?

Turns out, expert botanists do:
to plant bulbs, divide stalks, dig weeds—
it's a revelation, efficient beyond anything.
Easy to poke in, it unearths tough invasive roots.

Linked, my son and I, simpatico by nature already,
allied now by the garden tool we're both wielding,
removing creeping intruders, exorcising unnamed threats,
both psychic and botanical.

This chiseled dagger, this arcane tool,
this unheard-of soil knife, ties him and me
while his boy's voice links us with magical vibes.
Despite years and miles between us, we're joined
in the gardening passion, strong like his son's ABC's delivery.

Finding Their Way

My beautiful brainy athletic children
should find their way, now, while I can watch.
They should take hold of their excellent bold forays
but they dip and dive and hover in flux,
mired in the visceral agony of indecision,
in struggles they don't share over the phone.

Miles apart, I can see the jiggling leg,
the rolling eyes, intake of breath,
"I think I gotta go now," glancing away.

The expert cook has proved his mettle—
chopped and sautéed, grilled and puréed,
made sauces and glazes, pyramids and decorations,
used expert knives, worked twelve-hour days,
turned out exquisite, pricey delights,
but will he stay, get promoted, get a raise,
or join his buddies out West with no job in sight?

A brainy jokester, a quick study of Moby Dick, Richard Russo,
Presidential politics. A ski racer, trivia contest winner.
There's little he can't do or learn.
And what sympathies—hates to see 'sad fellows,'
loves all bears . . . and dogs and cats. A wonderment
to the grill guys who give him dicey clues to immigrant life.

The other one, doctor of plants, lover of green growing things,

champion yoyo meister, Congressional science fellow,
ski racer, artist, who made Halloween outfits for the younger:
a box, turned TV set, so his brother could be a talking head.
Art inhabits his life—watercolor sketches, pottery vases,
etchings of flowers and trees, all grace this house.

Hopes, like all mothers, for these extra-ordinary two
to find their way, to have their own
boy or girl to dress up on Halloween . . .

"Small but Brave"

My two were always shining flowers,
the heart and sparkle of our world—
with jokes and smiles and spirits high—
writers, painters, actors, athletes,
bold travelers, they invented lives
beyond this homespun repertoire.

Chef, botanist, comedian, potter—
they surprised us, were bigger,
more and better, faster and smarter
than the family paths or parent maps.

One bikes miles across a West Coast locale,
to work long into the night as bar chef
marshalling food stuffs into vats of hot oil
for *pomme frites, croque monsieur* and such.

The other, brilliant in science and art,
now, blue-eyed, handsome,
in a suit, he's turned to unfamiliar turf,
trapped in a long grind to somewhere,
like the biker, he perseveres.

Small no more, they have become
our long-forgot, storybook
small, brave tailor
who nailed five in one blow

and stitched "small but brave"
across his tailor's belt.

One of the Guys

Finger by the nose—
my two did that years ago
with gales of laughter and shouts of
'finger by the nose.'
Now it all jumps back to me,
the cavorting poking hollering.
They quick put a finger by the nose
for some kind of dibs,
for first or last or not-me in a game,
for some quick exemption,
to not clear the table
or mow the lawn, empty the garbage
or rake or something.
First finger by the nose
or noisiest claim thereof
gave the job over to the brother,
they shouted.

Now here comes a photo of
our lovely quiet grandbaby Max
just a few weeks past premature birth,
his pointing finger beside the nose—
asleep, adorable—
a personality already, himself,
linked to his dad and his funny uncle,
finger by the nose, to join the guys
as one of the guys

aligned, in sync, belonging to them
a promise and a wish
as he's just getting started.

He's got a ways to go our Max
before he joins the hilarity
of racing to the start,
bumping up against the raucous boyhood
that my two had together
and just may offer up in the genes
to our newborn baby wonder,
at home now with his new-minted parents,
learning together to be in the world of Max—
so strange, so new, and funny too.

Bits and Scraps of 'Littlehood'

Icons of my sons swim forth in this small house
that no longer shelters their spark, their whimsy,
their glimmering selves. But mounted on walls,
stashed in corners, packed in drawers and cabinets,
their things fill all the niches and spaces
with landmarks of littlehood (they called it).

Stymied in my lame attempts to sort,
I see visions emerge of Lego cities
strewn with Matchbox cars
and jungles of furry bears, tigers and monkeys
stalking cluttered boy-bedrooms.
Their touch, their efforts, their auras
reign forth in spiral notebooks, paintings,
spaceman sculptures. Each treasure
swims out and threatens to engulf me
in waves of remembered afternoons.

And so I cannot bring myself to jettison
the handmade art, comics, stacks of Wild Things
and Stuart Little's. I've harbored their stuff too long,
blaming them, while I'm the one can't bear to look
at books we shared about a pig floating skyward,
a king in a bathtub, the velvet rabbit, fantastic fox,
or brave friends, Amos the mouse and Boris the whale.

Of course I knew they would grow up
and move out. I watched it happen, collaborated,
helped them pack, shipped their bikes out west.
And felt a shock as the center of gravity
took up residence in a different time zone,
leaving only scratchy cell tones to connect us.

Now the coming visit home, along with a girl,
just might prompt a purge of littlehood's trappings,
and drive me headlong into new configurations
that turn loss into unfamiliar gain
well beyond these near-sacred
bits and scraps of memory.
I just might learn to join in, bake a cake,
and embrace their separate journeys.

"Ben's rented a robe," Dave said.

And so I took a trip for the ages,
like the other parents took
for his lab-mates from Thailand and China,
to celebrate those who deserve celebrating.

My first-born all smiles
should have flowers and toasts
ribbons and wine, kudos, huzzahs
after seven years of lab work
two marathon months of
all-through-the-night writing,
so The Committee would sign—
the last, biggest hurdle full done.

Alerted by chance three weeks before
by the canny sly smile of his brother.
"Ben's rented a robe," Dave said.
So I booked a flight and headed out west.

One could do no less to herald the day,
after his years of sunny California,
skiing in Tahoe, throwing pots,
yo-yoing down streets,
raising rescued plants and vines,
biking miles untold, catching movies and plays,

doing political door knocking—
a life of science, revved up with art,
paint, prints, plants, pottery—
now to be anointed
a man with three letters after his name.

He had filled his notebooks
week by week day by day
hour by hour with measurements
of how the sun damaged and the cells repaired
the magical DNA of Arabidopsis—
notebooks of numbers upon numbers.
Finally The Committee signed.
The seal was sealed.

And I showed up to witness the day.
Seated and proud, tearful and amazed.
Then there he was marching in, all a-sparkle,
in rented academic garb, floppy velvet hat,
fat gold tassel, three discreet stripes
on puffed pleated sleeves of a long black gown.
His name, his degree, his topic proclaimed.
Draped with ceremonial hood, applauded by lab mates,
embraced by soaring majestic Berkeley oak trees,
there he was—
Ben himself smiling smiling smiling in the sun.

The long ride home from a ski area

Silent suffering reigns, front and back
in the steamy car; skis and poles buckled
on top, boots and bags in the trunk.
Four of us motoring through the dark
away from the slopes,
down curved two-lane mountain roads,
steeply banked with snow on both sides,
heat pumping over wet skiers,
the air thick with attitude.

Nothing could jolly him out of the grim
sense of victory so close now lost.
He doesn't get out for snacks
at the after-race gas station depot
where noisy skiers crowd in
to consume cinnamon buns, chips,
soda, chocolates, egg rolls.

A gate missed at the end of the run
in the last race of the day—
the chance for a good finish,
gone in a tenth of a second.

Silence hangs heavy, words don't help.
We have to endure an endless

silent ride home and hope the reeking
disappointment, dashed hopes,
squelched expectations won't leave scars.
Can race after race done with such heart
turn into "life lessons"?

Doing wall-sits late on winter school nights,
building muscle strength and staying power
in a family with no great heritage in sports?
Immigrant grandparents knew Goethe, Mozart, Mahler,
hikes in the Alps or walks in the park, not American sports—
but we flooded their lives with Little League,
soccer, the Red Sox, college hoops.
They brought the heart
to train weekends, holidays, after school.

Grabbing a bag lunch, skis, boots, poles,
wax, goggles, sharpeners, shin guards, helmet, gloves,
sometimes they clambered out alone
in black early hours on Vermont's icy roads
to get to the ski area for rounds of training:
to run gates, hike back when you miss one
run gates, hike back, knees in, bend low,
turn early, get close, go fast, get it right.

Each weekend a race, another chance
to soar down the hill
in an aerodynamic, full-body suit,
bash the gates away
and sail through the course
on the straightest line
for a good finish, please God, on race day.

Criminal Happiness

Dave called to say
he'd gotten back to college in Maine.
He'd avoided the blizzard that
often attacks in the valley between
the Green and White Mountains.
Still, I could tell from his voice
he'd met something else.
Embarrassed, chagrined, he blurted it out—
a speeding ticket on Route 2 near Danville.
Oh my gosh, it's a speed trap. I've been there.
It's well known to the neighborhood.
I was so excited. I cursed that wretched sheriff
and told Dave he got caught exactly where I did,
driving the ladies to Maine last May.
Now we were linked by genes and by crime.
His ticket matched the one landed on me.
He wasn't the only victim or culprit or perp.
We were both of us innocent victims
nabbed by the sheriff of Caledonia County,
filling his quota of tickets.
Going ten miles over the forty-five limit—
while tractor trailers roared by unstopped—
had cost us each a hundred and eleven dollars.
How could that be?
And how could it mean happiness?
Both of us astonished at the duplicate rip-off
by the lyrical sheriff of Caledonia County.

Now Dave's feeling as happy as I,
surprised that his mother also got nailed.
His call uncovered something quite fine
a sweet correspondence in crime.

Tell-tale snapshots

He sent a gift that let me in
through glimpses
of a whole world opening—
an e-mailed picture essay
my son and his girl
on vacation, together.
'Jennifer's Picasa web album,
Readfield, Maine, August 2008'—
snapshots of their moments
out of business suits, into tee shirts
at ease by the smooth lake,
lilies, evergreens, grasses.

Him, at the water's edge
squinting at the sunset
paintbrush in air,
deft watercolor strokes caught
once on paper, once in pixels.
Her camera discovering him.
Him finding her by the lake,
looking back at him,
their rhythms emerging.

She found him yo-yoing,
pondering a fern, a plant with berries
a chipmunk, smooth mottled stones
by the water's edge,

then two Pabst cans at table
a meal in the rustic cabin.

Wordless, they let me into their world
as they let each other in, on vacation,
at the edge of a quiet lake, ducks floating past.
The loon's plaintive sound just barely audible
from here.

Glimpses

They flew to Nashville of all places,
Seattle-based son Dave and his New York City girlfriend.
He was to be in a friend's wedding; she up and joined him
for a fifth cross-country meet-up
in their three-month old romance—
quite a cinematic whirl, I'd say.
He gleamed from a photo in curly-haired glory.
She, smiling and beautiful in a flowing orange dress,
clung sidewise to his sharp tuxedo.

A photo of son Ben and his young son
building complex Lego structures
captured their rapport and concentration.
Another, from a seaside camping adventure,
revealed the same delight the dad once felt
exploring sea life, squiggly things in tide pools,
a beachside passion to share now with his boy.

Photo glimpses are what we've got.
Phones and Skypes and airlines help
but don't overcome this far-flung family diaspora,
don't offer hugs, romps, shared meals,
leisurely chats, hikes, meandering get-togethers.

Both sons, such handsome devils,
more or less fill our waking hours.
Grown and gone, they reside in our minds eye.

But, one hopes, we are not stuck like cinders in theirs.

Really, they just barely met

We counted the days till his visit,
hoped the best flowers would be blooming,
made the bed, filled the fridge, scrubbed stuff, got ready.

But the dad's jerry-rigged coffee machine exploded,
then he cut his hand harvesting cucumbers and took to bed.
I whipped up a gallon of gazpacho. Crazy was taking over.

Our son arrived from Seattle and jollied us to good sense,
peppered us with queries and jabs, joined us at concerts.
Then mid-week—The Girl arrived by surprise from New York

full of smiles, laughter and very good manners—
she brought a house gift!
They put us at ease with their own ease, smiling non-stop.

Good cheer flourished—their inside jokes, glances, high spirits,
homemade pasta from the son, adoring looks from The Girl,
their adventures around Burlington, The Fair, Al's French Fries

the pleasure of seeing them together,
their glowing, unfussy good looks—cinematic really:
his curly hair and bushy beard, her glorious thick black hair.

We stayed calm and well mannered (congratulations).
Early-week crazy vanished.
They joined us for meals in the garden.

We basked in their happiness and stayed out of the way except to grab a few photos. She sent one to her mom.

'Adele will like this,' she said.

Oh man, those ceramic bonsai pots!

shapes and sizes perfect
for curved stems, gnarly trunks
shiny green-topped plantings,
well known to aficionados
bonsai growers and pot-makers
who click hearts on his Instagram posts

daily my son reveals elegant pots
in varieties of size, shape, glaze,
rough or smooth or crackly sometimes
mame, yunomi, shohin, nanban—Japanese named—
ready to host a bonsai plant for years and years

Instagram posts let me see his work by stealth,
small pots, large ovals, an ikebana vase
once the blazing red-orange kiln fire
another day a group of just-fired pieces
sometimes outliers—a ceramic frog or menacing rat

each one, smooth or crinkled or ridged
glazed with chemicals and slips and fired,
rough crumbs filed from the bottoms
where clay feet and drain holes appear to nurture a plant

pulled from the fierce cauldron of kiln heat
with expertise of shape and color
density of clay, potter's wheel dynamics
chemistry of glazes, heat of firing
(avoiding 'irreparable stress cracks')
shaping ever more shapes
glazing ever more colors and finishes
firing ever more artfully crafted pieces

his comments: 'little painted guys,' 'a tiny angry owl,'
'misty Chinese mountains,' 'plum blossoms on a *shohin*,'
'I think I nailed the trout,'
'working the kiln is like being a coal man on a steam locomotive'

the bonsai artist creates his pots
then photographs, posts, sells, packages, and ships to bonsai fans
and I watch from afar in amazement

" 'preciate it, man," the President said.

Our Dave got the primo assignment,
a ten-minute one-on-one with President Obama--
just him, the President, the Secret Service, a photographer.

Hey Dave, how ya doin' man, the President said.
Dave kept breathing, shook hands, quaked,
but opened strong: *Fine, Mr. President.*
Then he asked a tough question about big Pharma.
At the end the President said, *'preciate it, man,*
shook Dave's hand, and was away.

Dave questions the willing and the unwilling,
does research, digs deep, crunches numbers,
writes page-one stories about the coal industry,
about chemical spills in the river of drinking water,
about meth labs and shuttered businesses, lobbyists and politicians,
about corruption and chicanery, and about heroism,
day after day—enterprise journalism, breaking news.

He mostly answers our calls, even on Saturday night.
How is it that one so sociable, so swamped with buddies
from high school to college to the restaurant kitchen
where he was the only Anglo invited to watch a TV boxing match
in the dishwashers' walkup flat,
or in college where his whole class cheered him at commencement

because he had famously defended his buddy
during a graduation high-jinx encounter with the law.

Now he's in a town that has yielded one good friend
who got a new job and moved away,
and a regular Sunday night dinner party
at the home of a couple as old as us parents.

A funny, talented guy, our Dave, who remembers poems,
who's the best reader of novels in a family of readers,
who's a skier, a biker who bikes to work,
and who also happens to be adorable cute.
Surely he's perfect to be plucked up
even in Charleston, West Virginia
by a cute smart girl who can, *'preciate it, man.*

Grandparents' Anthem: They're Coming!

And that takes center stage.
No worries that yellow is stalking
the tomato plants, spelling wilt or mildew or blight.
Or that it's raining again. And it's cold in July.
And the lying, profiteering, insulting horrors
continue apace from Trumpville.
All that can evanesce into nothingness
because—woo wooooo—they booked a flight.
Ben, Jenny, and little Max are coming!

Now clean the rooms, make the beds, vacuum.
Dust everything, vacuum again.
Unload the multiplying hordes of books in the guest room.
(Three boxes to the public library yesterday, more today and
    tomorrow.
Don't lose heart. Don't cling to memories stored in one book or
    another.
Who would re-read *Tristam Shandy* at this age?)

Mow the lawn. Weed the garden. Put flowers in vases.
Remember their favorite dishes. Plan meals.
Shop for the freshest best stuff.
Figure out an adventure for four-year-old Max
to see cows, pick flowers, splash in the lake,
show off his climbing prowess at the playground.

Make a cake. Make the beds. Get ready!

Because, all together now, they're coming!

Max arrived

We held him, sung to him, gazed at him,
amazed and struck quiet—to have a grandson.
That squiggle, that grimace,
that stretch from fingers to toes
arching back, pointing forward,
puckered lips that say something
or capture a bubble—
each tone, each twist—eloquent,
whether a burp, a sneeze, a poem.

His dad swooped into fatherhood
like a natural—awestruck himself,
ready with calm, sweet, deft handling.
He soothes the baby's cries
with his skill of a potter shaping pots,
his patience of a botanist
growing plants from tiny seeds.

I knew the dad to be graceful.
He swooped down a ski course
biked and ran and raced
for the love of motion.
But what a surprise to see him
with the babe in his arms,
on his shoulder, in his lap,
calmed into quiet
when the rest of us failed—a surprise gift

Backhoes and Cats

I'm settling in to age and place,
with ruffled feathers smoothed, at last, by letting go.

I'm accepting the wisteria won't bloom.
It shapes the patio, gives hideouts to chickadees and gold finch.

I'm letting go worry over neighbor cats
roaming the garden while we feed the birds.

I'm embracing gifts: bright cardinals at the feeder,
ice clinking in highballs, afternoon light licking over the garden,

Skyping with grandson Max, hearing his enchanting chuckles,
chatting with son Dave, reporting from Appalachia.

I'm practicing letting go small frets. I'm building resilience
to handle the inevitable big ones which will inevitably arrive.

I'm learning to let Ben, father of Max, husband of Jenny,
And Dave, out West, shape their worlds.

I'm practicing acceptance by letting go
my fixation on the assault on the green behind our house
now bedecked in backhoes and pounding machines. Horrifying.

Still, I admit I sometimes like the roaring industry of it all.

Passions of Dads and Boys

overlap, but don't always align
while connection yet glows from each to each

one grows seedlings, the other
fixes on Pokemon's furry oddballs

plants and ceramics—great loves of the dad
chess, baseball, basketball, absorb the six-year-old

the dad grows new life from seeds and sprouts
that push forth to stem, leaf, bud, flower

through winter under grow lights
till spring reprieve of full-bore outside light

the boy, nurtured and watered with dumplings, pancakes, books,
orchestrates Pokemon cards, chats with fuzzy toys Evie and Pikachu

multiplies the number of dots up and across
on the rectangles embedded at street crossings

the dad shapes ceramic bonsai pots and scary clay rats
the boy solves tricky wooden puzzles of space and logic

and the twosome, deep down connected with the mom,
enjoys the thrill of surprise:

triumphant Cub Scout home-built racing-car

An Uncanny Alert

I started on burgers, rolls, green beans
then joked I'd trade him a whiskey sour
for dinner making.
My son, the bona fide chef, home for a visit,
sidled up and set a plan in motion.

And turned out a surprising, primo meal:
vermicelli topped with Asian-flavored burgers
grilled, just so, carrots and kohlrabi, quick brined,
basil lettuce green beans
and perfect light-lime fish sauce.

Just as we sat down—a monster thunderclap,
a lightning bolt, closer, louder, bigger
than I'd ever seen or heard,
a bright white light right outside the door,
almost in the door,
so powerful the cat and I jumped across the room in tandem.

Was it a fearsome alert:
this rare interlude of summer dinner
with my son is fast fleeting.

It spelled a recognition:
my son on the cusp of change,
rumbling with talent, unleashed,
not yet tamed into a future,

home for this sweet brief intermezzo
and off to parts unknown

"Get Back Loretta"

sang the Beatles back in the day
when Dave, age four, and Ben, fourteen,
cavorted in the back seat
of the chartreuse Fiat rental car
as we rambled over dirt roads
into the deep wooded hills of rural Portugal.
Ben pushed Dave back and back
with a hearty shove, shouting
"Get Back, Loretta, Get Back."

Dave chortled with a daring, 'Ha,'
and bounced seat-beltless (there were none)
up and up again in jolly defiance.
Now his tenacious challenging core
prevails 25 years later in a reporter's world
where he digs deep, again and again.
And Ben's care-giving instinct
shapes him, always an artist
now a dad, too, watching a toddler
bounce up and back, over and again.

"Get Back Loretta" swept into my lonesome kitchen
in a Beatles' radio marathon New Year's Day—
I'll go with the spirit of the lovable foursome,
conjuring Ben and Dave in the back seat,
pushing and guffawing, one elegant, one raucous,
moving ineluctably towards the future.

Next song up, perfect for a new year,
a lesson, a heads-up to be grabbed
and hoped, for my own lovable twosome:
"It's get-ting bet-ter all the tiiime."

Our Own Liturgy

a High Holiday walk, now without our sons,
yet in balmy fall weather, radiant with the ache of evanescence,
leads down a favorite road deep into the multi-colored countryside,
hills glowing a symphony of yellow, orange, salmon, magenta,
outcroppings of rock for percussion, evergreens for harmony,
framed by stark majesty of Mt. Mansfield

the boys' presence felt all around,
memory flashes of snowy drives to skiing
with boots and bags and bundles and snacks,
the air sweet now with cedar and pine,
apple trees proffer ripe fruit
scenes of our two batting apples down the road with sticks

instead three sheep, wearing
curved-horn shofars to honor the season,
stand, staring, at the edge of the fence
in their bold incurious way

a horse rolls around, feet in the air,
scratching, finally righting himself,
like a child getting things straight
after stumbling attempts

a man pulls out dahlia bulbs
for replanting next year
along the edges of his well-kept house,

caring for things in seasonal course

then fallen chestnuts, smooth mahogany shiny
like fat rosary beads unscripted for the Days of Awe,
visions of our two collecting pockets full
for tune-makers in shook metal buckets.

The seasons and the years soften
in the presence of these hillsides,
the bounty of the mountains,
this ceremonial walk, our liturgy
shaped by sons around whom
our days and lives are remembered

Family Heritage

Borscht

That magenta happens only in a white bowl
of grated beets quickly boiled, set before you—

a wonderment of color
topped by a dollop of thick white sour cream

garnished by bright green sparkles of chives—
your own startling dish of color and taste.

Redolent of earth,
a bulbous root that never saw the sun,

pulled full grown by its leafy airborne top
from perpetual dark below ground

where its crinkled seed burst,
grew to seedling with slim filament of root and

two-pronged dicotyledon of emerging leaves,

swelled into round heavy beet,
stalks of red-veined frilly greens reaching for the sun.

How else could it taste but earthy?
Its brief life housed entirely in soil.

Hearty peasant food that fed families through the years—

Eastern Europe's heritage of borscht

with cabbage and without, a meaty shin bone sometimes,
onions, carrots, parsnips, turnips, potatoes—root crops all

redolent of more than earth, of crowded rooms full of prayer,
unspeakable hardships escaped, good fortune claimed.

A birthright to pull out of the earth and make into soup.

Bee and Jules

Caught fast in full swoon, hooked—
no matter her immigrant family,
Jews too observant for his exquisite taste,
himself a scholar, taste-maker, sporting fellow—
he fell full force, one look,
a goner, never to love any other.

A brash young man, maybe twenty years old,
bowled over forever by a dark-eyed beauty
who noticed his ways, fancy and showy,
but it happened to her the same—caught, a goner.

So they took his Model T on a snowy cold night—
went and got married, eloped. Then nowhere to go
but home to the bakers, her rowdy folks, all lodged together
in one crowded house, siblings, spouses and babies.

* * *

Citified and dandified, he'd never seen the like—
a scene alive with big ovens,
slings for rising, racks for cooling—
challah, mandelbrot, honey cake, rugelach.

They put her fellow to work
scraping and scouring scorched bread pans.
That had to rankle, had to smart
one so fancy, so brainy, so fine,

turned to a lowly kitchen scrub. . . .

* * *

Fed up, cocksure, he squashed a cigarette
on his dinner plate, on the Sabbath, *en famille*—

He'd affronted, confronted, insulted her family.
That did it, tied him to bread pans forever.
He knew he should go. His learning demeaned,
along with his elegance, his suits and his pipes.

He packed up his bride and his baby girl too
and headed down South to an alien land
for a fifty-year marriage of children,
grandchildren, Sabbaths and pets.

She never quite tamed the fancy young man
who held on to his high flown tastes,
flourished in business, in travel,
learning and style—Stravinsky, Joyce,
a well-tied tie even on weekends,
while she shaped a big, flower-filled house,
serving up bountiful dinners
for family, neighbors and guests.

The legacy started with that brash cocky young man
swept away by his beautiful bride
lives in us offspring, striving forever for a ride
on a rumbling, rambling, new-fangled, fanciful Model T.

Mystery Hegemony

Orphaned at twelve, my dad, when his mother died.
His alcoholic father no factor, it seems.
Grandparents—called Ma'-ma and Pa'-pa—
took him to China (his ivory-tiger souvenir
stood mute on the shelf through my childhood years).
Those dignified Victorians who peer stern-faced
from a really large photo, became the parents, I guess,
them and McBurney Prep in lower Manhattan
and Aunt Bertha Cone's Blowing Rock estate
for summers with his horse called Lucky.
About them all, we know little.

As the fourth child, I saw him carry on with gusto—
high-flown tastes, NYC at the Waldorf for deals
and always good manners. Always a well-tied tie.
One business and then another, never losing heart:
photo-copying before xerox, plastics—that was big, chemicals.
The stolid, keep-moving, post-war, robust fifties and sixties.
He lodged us in the big white house up the hill
where she gardened and cooked to a fare-thee-well.
We knew flush times and South Carolina summer heat.
He'd bound up the stairs to kiss mother
and get served endless gourmet meals.
We took him to the airport for business trips
when air travel was rare.

A man on a mission who loved his wife

and his family—but was not distracted by it all.

Did he take up all the room, breath all the air from our growing up?

Or did he just blindly try to make it possible?

The Family Diamond

adorned four brides of much-loved sons
over four generations,
travelling, in sickness and health,
across the Atlantic from Gotha on the Elbe
to Sherman Oaks on the Pacific,
across the American continent,
to Kew Gardens, then Merrick,
north for forty years in Vermont,
and now southward to Maryland.

From mothers-in-law to daughters-in-law,
the diamond ring moved from hand to hand,
first in luxury, then hardship,
in rapid flight from the Holocaust onward to America,
a century and more of travels,
thus to me, hippie, feminist, activist.

A classic big sparkler with two baguettes,
the solitaire began in high-collared Old-World elegance
adorning the hand of the matriarch in a manor house full of books
        and music,
thrust into émigré acclimation, the bombast of striving America in the
        forties
where the ring was passed to my own mother-in-law, once of
        Mannheim,
then New York, sales girl at Macy's, bride of a gutsy German refugee
who joined the U.S. Army to fight the Nazis.

Now to me, wife of their son, both of us '60s activists,
meeting, marching, sitting-in for Civil Rights, protesting Vietnam;
it came to me, for whom a diamond seemed a disconnect.
Yet, how quickly I grew easy with the glow, the statement, the size,
the way it says whatever it says, a mute megaphone.

Last year I gave it to my own daughter-in-law,
a brainy scientist, mother of our grandson.
I admit I sometimes miss it as it takes its rightful journey
from mother-in-law to daughter-in-law
along the mythic voyage in a story felt by each pair,
a tale embedded in the drifts of love and competition, for the son.

Together we inhabit the realm of mothers of sons,
marveling over baby Max, who, one day, may draw a bride
into the legendary circle
of the well-travelled family heirloom diamond ring.

His own rhythm

That way that he had
of descending the stairs
that galumphing step—
odd for such a light man
ba-dump, ba-dump
never varied—ba-dump ba-dump
on each step.

He bounded ahead
with adventures, adventuring
bringing home gifts,
doing this and that business
succeeding, failing, succeeding again.
Undaunted,
map-making, plastics, chemicals, professoring—
no realm too foreign or new.
Through the decades the spirit held fast
whatever the climate, setbacks, chagrins—
ba-dump ba-dump on the stairs.

When the son rebelled
stole a cake off a teacher's desk
was in-your-face surly assertive,
the father wanted fine manners.
We girls looked on bemused
in silence or sweet conversation
around standoffs of father and son.

The father ascending descending
ba-dump ba-dump, each step,
while a fraught family world
swirled around him
seen or altogether unseen

Shrimp Cocktail

Maybe Thai or Vietnamese workers
did the sticky work of cleaning these shrimp:
slit the backs, remove the black line,
keep the tail intact, deliver the crustacean in one plump piece—
leaving me to remove legs and shells

and to drift into long lost visions of Pawley's Island half a century ago

where Fillomon, a man of Gullah origins, walked the beach
singing lyrical sounds that told my mother
fresh shrimp, flounder and more were at her kitchen door.

Beach days flooded into mind . . . when we kids went crabbing
on the creek side, not the ocean side, of the island.
Happy at the freedom, we clambered up the ladder
and out a long dock bridging the creek marsh,
proud to traverse rickety wood slats over shadowy waters.
We hauled along a pail of chicken bones for bait,
vowing to bring back crabs for dinner,
then spent the long afternoon on the dock—
a world removed, no grownups, no shoes, barefoot toes,
no school, no time table, snacks in sacks,
just there to drop a bone on a string into water swirling with sea life,
skittering bugs, wafting seaweed, unknown mysteries.

We peered down and waited for the crabs to bite
then scooped them into our nets, sometimes three or four at once,

till we filled our pails with squirming flailing claws,

and, as the sun went down, carried them, live,
to our sandy-floored beach house on stilts
set between the creek and the ocean
with glories all around, and dangers too.

That evoked the long-forgotten story
of Fillomon taking my older brother and sister
for a special treat to ride in his boat on the creek.
But catastrophe: they were all three
swept out into the wide open waters of the ocean
beyond the safety of the shallow, slow-moving creek.
Somehow tragedy was avoided. They got back.
Only the tale of terrifying near-calamity was passed down.

What did my mother endure—her children at sea in Fillomon's boat?
Ancient Gullah-speaking Fillomon must have seemed a practiced
        seaman
familiar with tides and currents on the Pawley's Island Creek.

Most of the players now gone,
but that creek
that beach house
that crabbing off the dock
that tragedy averted—
all swept into mind
as I peeled shrimp for, of all things, a Super Bowl party.

Sons in the Family Soup

His ever-mounting antic ploys
from youth to work to marriage—
a brainy, disheveled, big-hearted guy,
my brother was always somehow
slightly out of sync.

All her life and his, our mother struggled
to catch, cover for, bolster and bundle out the door,
the son of great promise, the awkward stumbler,
the good-natured, in-your-face jokester,
amongst three sisters who were always good
turning him therefore otherwise.

She made his favorite foods,
visited his teachers when his hi-jinks
caused headaches or tears, quelled
the uproar when his mushrooming antics,
spills, elbows on the table disrupted
the staid family dinner
where deep down flowed
the primal need to best the father.

But our Victorian patriarch,
suited up with his well-tied tie and
well-shined shoes conducted
the dinner hour like a religion.
She watched her curly-headed son,

baked pies, rolled pastries,
layered chocolate cakes for his pleasure.

My own mystery son, his sweetness, style, quiet wit—
so different from the uncle—
yet both may have the father in their mind's eye.

We offer carbonara and kugel
like she offered black walnut pie
and great roasts of beef half a century back.
Mine, full of art and whimsy,
paints garden watercolors,
delves deep into plant science,
runs, like his uncle, in all weather,
skis with the grace of a gazelle,
elegant, poetic, artistic,
no in-your-face jokester like my brother.

Yet my nights match hers decades later,
as I watch the brilliant son,
gauge each clue, each telephoned snippet
that twirls like a weathervane display
of his barometric pressure.

The circular mind-swim repeats,
afloat in the opaque mystery of another self,
first born sons, reflections despite all,
of our own inclinations
as the years mount up around us
and the family soup boils down.

Stroke

I offer cup to mouth
like she did for our mother
her lips pursed to pull in
cleansing waters,
touch, strength, health, relief

my sister needs the help now
to sustain life, to connect
to know we're there
to know her self
the self she knew so well
the self she's hunting for

perhaps we all come to this—
some infirm, needy shape or other
but the shock of one so close
so spirited, who never seemed old

to see her, to be her
to be bed bound, to feel tied down
to believe they tied you down at night
to take such a blow

she will move beyond it
she does so hour by hour
madness and will, confusion and intent
all push her forward, bit by bit and leap by leap—

she whispered, 'the applesauce has little to recommend it'
she has not lost her self

today she fed her self with her good hand
then used the good one to move the still one
and so she pushed and stood on the good leg
waiting yet for use of the other

laid low but not undone
she has the mind
more mind than muscle now, but the will
to teach the deaf muscle to hear
to listen to respond to know
to have the instinct
to do what her ceaselessly thinking brain
tells the muscle to do
to get her self back
to rebuild to regain
to reconfigure
her life

About my brother

His shortened life will never be okay.
His sons—bolstered by his furious love—
are like circus gymnasts circling a grand brown bear
trying to please
like he circled our father, trying to please.

A high school football wannabe,
he made us little sisters into practice guards.
That always ended badly in calamitous noise
foretelling calamity to come.

He stole a cake from the teacher's desk.
He stashed his spit-polished cordovans in the fridge
to keep them ceremonial
for graduation and the midshipman event.

The brother with three sisters.
Sons ten years apart,
each the world to him,
each trying to please, needing to escape.
One a professor, engineer,
like the grandfather his father could never please.
The other, a champion wrestler.

Both orphaned, way too young,
they circle and circle the grand brown bear
who had one wife and then another,

who came and went and came again
and always a girl in between.

'I guess I ate one too many jelly doughnuts,' he said,
in bed in that stark white hospital room
treated by a drip of morphine.
'I could get out of bed right now and paint this room.'
And then he was gone.
A great presence, gone
way too soon.

Closing the Gap: Paean to the Post Office

I thought I'd erase the gulf between us,
reconnect with glitter in a box.
But my erstwhile birthday gesture went awry.

Sisters two years apart—once clothed in childhoods'
starched and ironed matching dresses,
we waited for the bus with our tokens and snacks,
went to Girl Scout camp, took piano lessons,
shared a room with twin beds in fluffy skirts,
and whispered secrets, miles and years ago.

I'd send something of turquoise shimmer
held on gold stems to frame her hair and match her eyes.
But I misaddressed the well-wrapped gift,
meant to celebrate an important birthday.

Then, a blessed notice came:
"An envelope needed pick-up at the PO."
Who knew the PO would take that package to Santa Monica,
try to find her, explain in notes they couldn't,
bring it back to Burlington, Vermont.

Imagine the hands and sacks and stations,
airplanes and rolling carts that package felt,
tripping across the continent and back.

I stood in line, watched them retreat to the back room,
beyond the beyond of the PO counter,
to retrieve the small packet covered with scribbles:
"Tried, unknown at this address."
I re-packed it. Put on the right address,
delivered it to the counter, and sent it off again.

Today's her actual birthday.
The mega relief of the once-missing gift arrived—
and she loves the earrings.
And the stark, unwelcome gap between us has clearly shrunk.

A Child's Glimpse Half a Century Later

She so beautiful in glitter and scents,
silk scarves, strappy shoes,
sparkling eyes, amazing smile;
him, dapper, proper, always suited out,
quietly beaming passion for her.

A stylish couple, charming, light, clever.
Without us four they could be free,
glamorous, on the town,
if only for one late night in fancy dress.

Where could they have gone
In that deep south 50s world?
A jiving juke joint in the country
that only the hip would know?
Or a ballroom with a big band?

Now I see their one-night's glamour
without us quarrelsome children,
a chance to regain their kick-up-your heels,
flapper-style pre-Depression fun.

He could waltz. She did a mean Charleston
in rare moments round the kitchen.
He always bounded, loud, up the stairs

for a home-from-work smackeroo kiss.

What must those nights have held
in that grown-up glittering world
away from home
out of the clutches of a big worrisome family.

Seder Connections

We squoze round the table
in the townhouse of a cousin
in her seventh decade
along with son and his girl,
nephew and his new wife.

We twelve found our way
across town or country
brought gifts and good spirits
and gathered in a sociable,
secular mode.

Half the assembled
not steeped in the tradition
embraced it still this night
to hold out—against the dying of the light.

We embraced the ancient script
in the Haggadah of lyric Baskin watercolors—
lambs and robins, parsley, eggs and hope
patriarchs, pansies, oxen and tulips,
yearnings after spring.

We honored messages of hardship,
smiting of first-born, parting the waters,
escape to freedom.
Let it be so, we intoned, for those yet enslaved.

Two small girls lilted forth in Hebrew,
out of their mixed tradition
of nature, Torah, Jesus and Om—
a fine surprise that sparked the gathering.

We chanted the prayers, ate the symbols—
Hillel sandwich of matzoh,
horseradish, apple-nut charoses,
the mortar between the bricks,
the agony of the hauling.

We drank the wine four times,
chanted and chortled as the hours passed,
sang Dayaneu, An Only Kid,
downed gefiltte fish, matzoh balls,
tsimmes, broccoli, brisket.
Kept reading, kept going, found
the hidden *afikomen*,
before the girls faded to sleep.

We recalled seders in other houses
of matriarchs and patriarchs,
central players now missing,
crystal and daffodils, dogs under the table.
Remembered and remembered.
Parents, siblings, cousins.

We did it for my son, his girl,
my sister, her husband,
my nephews, their wives,
the girls who spoke Hebrew
and made us keepers of the glue
that binds these connections
year by year by year.

Poems from Our Climate

Gladiolas

maligned as funereal
an armload of gladiolas
makes an old lady alluring,
young again

left for weeks in the rain
discovered today
profusions of blossoms
overblown, exuberant,
out of control, falling akimbo
yearning to be cut, shown off

when placed in a vase
dignity returns, glory,
grace beyond imagining
lilting this way and that

each tall spike a statement
oranges grouped together
pink-tinged whites,
elegant, beyond description

turn over the soil
put bulbs in the ground
pull weeds, don't pull weeds
eight summer weeks later
profusions of gladiolas arrive

if children could be planted
nurtured, weeded
left out in the rain
left to their own devices
they'd be tall, spiky, glorious gladiolas too

Now the Permafrost is Melting

and warming the planet at a rate as yet unforeseen.
You'd think we'd hear the doomful toll
and finally pay attention to the catastrophe
we've wrought. We're just one kind
in nature's world of polar bears, big cats,
hippos, dolphins, cardinals, dragon flies,
lizards, tulips—all evolved, intertwined, awesome.

Whence came the birthright to wreak such havoc,
drive so many cars, dismantle mountaintops,
haul out the coal, set it afire
and send masses of planet-warming fumes into the air?
Wherefore the right to despoil and despoil again,
to watch the slow creep turn to a fast onslaught
of melting melting melting?
                    And now the permafrost.
Who ever considered the permafrost,
which has, it seems, risen to the top of the list
of indicators, of no-turning-back signs
that we have let loose the irreversible—
the rising of seas, the flooding of Mumbai
the sinking of coastal Bangladesh.
What of all the great seaport cities,
New York, Boston, London, Shanghai, Tokyo,
Miami? What of Vermont's maples

in red and orange and gold
that won't turn brilliant colors in warmth?
What of our bountiful seas, fished out,
choked, despoiled with floating plastic?

It's well past time to get real, to reverse the tide,
to halt the disappearance of the world
we lucky oldsters have enjoyed
while wreaking a legacy of damage
on our singular planet Earth.

Musing on the Animals

In the emptiness of winter
no surprise fox crosses
the once green expanse out back,
showing a quick glimpse
of elegant red-brown tail
then out-stretched, leaping, gone.

No lumbering woodchuck,
bane of the neighborhood,
explores with aplomb,
devouring sunflowers, zinnias,
snapdragon seedlings.

One lone mid-winter birdcall before dawn
suggests something ill-timed.
A solitary cat lopes down our ice-crunched street.

I wish I could rescue the animals
bring them home, sit them down to dinner
especially the horses, the tragic Barbaro
winner of the Derby, irreparably broken
two weeks later in the Preakness.
He should have been a Belgian
or a Clydesdale, supported on solid hooves
like squat paint cans with ruffles.

Ever more Barbaros, over-bred Arabians,

are fated to run for money on slim, two-year old legs,
instead of growing older, slower, evolving into Belgians
with rounded chestnut flanks
big beautiful heads, untold power—
but without racehorse elegant, death-defying speed.

Catastrophes Circle the Globe (October 2005)

It's season-ending zinnias, cosmos,
snapdragons and one fine rose, right here,
as catastrophes circle the globe.
Agony ravishes Kashmiri forests.
The dead in such numbers it means nothing.
We can't look. We look and can't see.
Brave photographers capture stretchers,
collapsed towers, endless piles of rubble,
trying to make us see
then they capture a hole in the rubble
live eyes imploring up through the hole
rescuers stymied. How to avoid a collapse?

On top of that—
mudslides bury a town in Guatemala.
A child trapped. They vow not to lose her.
Has her voice stilled? Did they get there?

Seventy thousand still wait in Louisiana shelters.

Places rich with plant life, orchids, hibiscus, ferns
flush with colorful birds, parrots, peacocks
kingly animals—elephants, tigers, ocelots, monkeys
tasty sea creatures—crabs, clams, oysters and shrimp.
Places cursed with lyrical names

Kashmir, Guatemala, New Orleans
now stand for horrors untold and the people trapped—
while we enjoy unearned, uncertain, blessed good fortune?

Early Lilacs Bloom and Oil Flows (2010)

Scent and shade of lilac blossoms
wafting atop sturdy branches,
year after year a lush new array,
this time weeks early. They burst full
right along with tulips, whose brilliance
should march the season forward, solo,
in stark reds and yellows. Now what?
With this untoward climate,
this warmth too soon,
will peonies still emerge
in plush seasonal glory in their course?

No matter. These puny dislocations
don't figure in a world upturned
by the horrific assault now swirling
in elegant deadly swirls
over once sustaining ocean waters
towards the Gulf's white sand beaches,
poisoning fish and pelicans,
shrimp and osprey,
slouching towards New Orleans,
our heart-breaking, blues-filled
musical home caught again
in the path of catastrophe.

Who can name the giant sea turtles,
ancient, heroic, swimming in oil,
without weeping? Who can think
of oysters, sifting and sifting
with their magical means and
never ridding their salty slippery selves
of oil. This, atop the disaster
that swept away neighbors
who made music on the front porch,
who dwelt with grace in The Big Easy
and then got ousted to Texas.

Survivors wait on porches, again,
watching the relentless slick
slide towards shore. The birds,
the marshes, the salty fecund brine
cloaked in ruination
and nothing halts the advance.

Some bizarre concrete lid
is lowered into the depths
to shut it off. Right. Not likely.
We watch TV screens of
telltale murky waters,
breathe in the scent of lilac,
and weep to tell the tale.

A Category Five, 8-29-05

What can it mean to my two Gospel ladies,
to all the singers of the Saint Peter Claver Gospel Choir?
They all live worship sing and work
right down in the middle of New Orleans
where a Category Five is headed straight for them
for the pews, the basement, rehearsal space, altar
for the whole assembled congregation
which can't now assemble
but has to evacuate, head for high ground.

But high ground is what New Orleans lacks.
It's banked itself on below-sea-level sweet sultry places
of music and food, jazz and gospel and trombones.
Random disaster can strike any place
but the Big Easy would never be ready to flee.
It's always known it lived on catastrophe waiting to happen
below sea level with locks and levees and lakes and the Gulf
and all manner of jerry-rigged man-made jimmying of the waters.
And besides, there lies the great big Mississippi River
scooched this way and that by the Army Corps of Engineers
when they thought they could manage the river, the ocean
the tides, the influx and outflow.

And now look.
Below sea level and what will happen to the Choir
to the pastor, to the Bishop Perry Middle School
to all the Black boys in white shirts and neat ties,

the inner city boys getting a leg up at Bishop Perry--
their mammas so hopeful and proud
and here comes a Category Five.

Conference-land on the West Coast

We landed in irrigated Southern California,
America's primo land of opportunity:
palm trees, eucalyptus, yachts in the harbor,
hotels and highways, no eateries nearby,
nothing to walk to, everything a cab ride away.

The hotel teemed with marketers
tweeting, texting, setting locales
on their GPS's, Foursquare, Gowalla,
placing themselves in bulls-eye circles
of friends they have friended.

Six hundred brainy conferees,
laptops and smart phones aglow,
prezzis and power points quietly humming,
smiling consultants and vendors bequeathing trinkets—
shades from Google, smart sticks from Fuse
click pens everywhere, a free drink each night.

All of it suited to my sons,
one twenty-something, one thirty-something,
while I'm the unlikely player
posited in this fertile swirl
of West Coast conferencing,
swimming upstream, faking it, keeping up, observing.

a cat and a dog

in this climate of catastrophe
earthquake, tsunami, radiation poisoning
I sit, cat purring next to me
husband-made muffins coming for breakfast
orchid blooming nearby with dancer's elegance
coffee perfect, space-heater toasty

but the dog in Japan who sat
his paw atop his injured friend
his journey back and forth
to rescuers, to his friend, to rescuers
till help came—
that dual survival, that faithful beast
amidst unspeakable deaths—
the stalwart heart-breaking devotion
the stoic outreach, the quiet dignity

yet these world-disrupting disasters
singular and planetary
have not, luckily, today in Mid-March 2011
undone my own sweet world

soaking rain

lightning streaking, thunder crackling
rain soaking deep to roots
the vegetable garden bursting into finale of bountiful gifts
one last ripening of tomatoes, cucumbers, zinnias

but rain in the Bahamas
like nothing ever before—a horror
terrifying, destructive endless
no one knows how to survive or rescue anyone
everyone caught
without food, shelter, clothing
without without, it's all without

our rain mocks their devastation
sets leaves glistening
fronds and flowers and fruits shining
but theirs . . .
shock, confusion, loved ones missing
gardens ruined, trees downed, homes flattened
flooding, endless debris and worse

and the horses on Chincoteague Island, turtles in the Bahamas

It's the people children everyone threatened
but we're not all there is.
We think we're all.
We delve into metaphysics

Music
Science
Poetry

But animals need space for their lives
realms we hardly understand
and trees that give life and breath and beauty

Still, the unimaginable horror:
for the people of the Bahamas

Hopeful Gardening

I head outside as soon as it's warm
to set myself adrift in something else.
Even wet leaves, harsh sticks
dried dank bits call me out.
I'm searching for escape from the news
left shouting on the breakfast table.
Today worse than ever
screams the bravado the macho crap
the mindless Trump ratcheting up
towards worldwide disaster,
taunting unpredictable North Korea.

I need the garden cure:
its lure of green to come
its pushing up of small hints
its numb nudgers (we used to call the promises),
the pod beneath a seed cap, budding buds,
crocus dotted in unexpected places.
Wind-spread spores have surprised us
with purple, white, yellow minnow-shaped blossoms
mid-lawn, speaking color in small flares.

The perennials, the summertime glories
still weeks away but moving fast
thrusting green shoots upwards
through last year's wet leaves
that I lift off to behold their promise

and escape the news.

Yesterday we marched and shouted
'Show us your taxes.' 'We want to know.'
We wore our pink pussy hats
of January's anti-Trump protests.
Today I'm hiding in the garden
hoping for relief in the escape zone.
But there's no escape in this climate of threat and bombast
from a shameless president, recklessly
seeking only his unknown unlearned selfish desires.

That Hallowed Space

Chinese students back in the '60s
circled the great round reading room
of the British Museum then stood quietly
behind the seat where Marx wrote—
groups of them would show up most days
quiet, soft-stepping, clad in drab gray overcoats,
wearing glasses and cropped hair
occasional whispering, staring
at the place where he'd sat,
or maybe just circled the room
since no one knew exactly where,
but knew he sat in the British Museum.

Those students peopled my months in the scholars' domain.
Librarians brought me oversized bound periodicals
a century old so I could discover
what George Eliot's peers thought of *Middlemarch*—
and sit in a wooden chair worn smooth over decades by serious folks,
with lamp light illuminating my assigned space,
big unwieldy books piled around me on one of the long desks
that spiraled out in radials through that great domed room.
I circled her sober insights while Chinese students at the periphery
searched for the meaning of Karl Marx's guide to life.

"We Are One" Concert, January 2009

The Boss, Beyoncé, Stevie Wonder,
the resplendent red-clad hundred-plus
female Gospel voices from somewhere,
the DC Gay Men's Chorus

the stars were there
and a million or two of us
cheering and high-five-ing
all along the dusty mall
before Abraham Lincoln
seated in his memorial.
All of us filled with wonder
at the wonder of it all.

The legacy of Lincoln echoed
in words and images of FDR, JFK,
King's eightieth birthday,
Rosa Parks, Langston Hughes,
Barbara Jordan and Frederick Douglas.

No bumps from the milling crowd
or waits to hold our standing place
or mounting chill in the cold or lost glove
could lessen the fact that we were there.

There for the new era of Obama
an era of hope and energy
despite fears about money,
wars in the Middle East,
tensions in India and Pakistan
unease for our children.

We were lifted up. We witnessed
the artists declaiming for us all
Denzel, Queen Latifah, Tiger Woods
Tom Hanks and Aaron Copeland,
Renee Fleming's soaring soprano,
Garth Brooks, U2, Shakira, Sheryl Crow
with high-heeled electric vibe.

Pete Seeger, the American spirit,
leader of movements for generations,
singing Woody Guthrie's
once-subversive anthem
"This land is your land, this land is my land"

and it crept up and sunk in:
this is a great country of rare spirit and talent
and hawkers of tee shirts, buttons, posters, caps
all along the streets of the Capitol,
three miles of which we walked to avoid gridlock
but gridlock descended at security gates where we
came to a halt because this great country happens also
to own more guns that any civilized state ever should . . .

But the air sparked electric with spirit and high fives
for the new first family who had arrived
with their own electric vibe.
We cheered for him who bears the staggering

weight of our times, and all were buoyed up
by the triumph on that day
of music, dance, song and art

Hakkapelittas

Insulation blown into the walls last summer
girds the house against cold this winter.
Gloves, hat, long johns, boots, coat
called into action.

Clear the walk, shovel the drive, eke out a path,
be wary of treacherous ice patches,
heave it, pile it, mound it and slog on.
The chill is back, more than remembered.

The good news—blessed bounty of snow tires
that splay moisture outward, the salesman said,
grip tight to a road mucked deep with slush.
I'll have them bronzed for the mantle-piece
loved like a child's first pair of shoes,
these Hakkapelittas. Decades in Vermont,
now my first real snow tires—transforming
like a birth, a new beginning. Just in time.

I rise up amazed at the cover of whiteness
blanketing the roof of each house,
muffling clatter, sending chickadees and sparrows
to perch prettily at the feeder.
A soft embrace takes over,
erasing gravelly clumps and grungy blots
silencing all in a wide vista of untouched whiteness,
a merging of sky and ground

inked with bare maple branches
like delicate arteries and veins,
evergreens painted with fluffy white scarves,
all the elements calling us to wonder and to awe—

and safe driving ahead.

We can't stop it, again (2004)

beautiful fat two-year olds
push their small-wheeled carts
wobbly and wild
one certain, the other yearning and trying
parents hovering
our idyllic street a gathering place
congenial, upbeat, sunny
where gardens and children grow
what about streets of Fallujah, Chechnya, Baghdad, Rwanda
like Mylai and the Mekong Delta
forty years ago

how can this happen again—
peaceful quiet for some
body parts and children dead
hellish discord and horror half a world away

we marched on Washington
ranted to overwrought parents
gave speeches, organized
felt outraged to be the lucky ones
but couldn't stop the napalm
our 'leaders' sent

now our 'leaders' don't care what havoc they send

our soldiers again caught dead center
hot, sick, scared
with no way out
and we can't stop it
again

Volunteers

The garden's uninvited guests
bring their own exact leaf, bud, stalk, flower—
pushy, hard to uproot, fast growing
tall and leggy, at home before you even know them:
seeds of last year's plantings,
a renegade tomato amongst the zinnias,
a stalky sticky humorous pink cleome edging out cosmos,
sweet peas crowding and clinging on cucumber vines,
sidling up close, making friends with a gladiola.

And the gladiolas—volunteering two strong plants
from each of last year's bulbs,
delivering two spikes of brilliant pink or full-throated yellow.
Also, beware rambling wild dill—
bushes of edible presence, everywhere,
sprouting feathery leaves and frilly yellow seedpods.

The most robust invader, arugula, AKA rocket,
crowds the nasturtiums and snapdragons with abandon, offering
        a more complex spice and bite
than the cultivars, giving plenty of tastes
full of nutrition of unknown, but certain value.
And of course, mint's back, shouting refreshing flavor,
calling for a Middle Eastern specialty or Southern alcoholic pleasure!

In and around all the deliberate vegetables and flowers,
volunteers compete with snapdragons, beets, peppers,

green beans, tomatoes, squash. Yet they teach us
to embrace surprise, to persevere, to learn devil-may-care assertion.

Autumn Harvest: A Romance

carrots potatoes beets onions—
hearty root crops
for the long haul of winter ahead
to nourish like a well-worn marriage
through short days and dark nights
with warmth of stews and stirrings

in the low glowing light of early fall
second plantings come full growth
beans, lettuce, arugula, aubergine—
the love-apple, tomatoes
a final outpouring of lush pleasures
before the plants wither and go dry.

gazpacho, sautéed leeks atop polenta
corn every day every which way—
fritters, on the cob, in pudding
one ear only per stalky plant,
an unseemly botany evolved for taste,
feed grain, hominy, all the uses
and abuses of high fructose
but we chomped off the kernels
row by row by row, and then another ear

the season's outpouring of pleasures—

apples, plumbs, nectarines, cider, raspberries
miraculous—so sweet, so varied, so distinct
succulent plenty in the face of catastrophe
in once-fertile countries all around the globe
It could take your appetite away
if the bounty weren't so luscious and ready
like a lover late in life.

Forget-me-nots

opened today despite cold,
spreading blue dots
in casual unhurried array
across the hillside.
Purple cone flowers—
nothing but mounds,
lilies—just spikes inching up.
But the blue-dots of forget-me-nots
are having their day,
spreading with abandon
everywhere.
I could pull them out
stop their encroaching
but those five-petaled
yellow-centered tiny
blue, white, everywhere blossoms
are too sweet to remove.
They will prevail
even when I pull them out
to give space to bee balm, peonies, roses.
Forget-me-nots will smartly
drop their seeds
everywhere
promising to return.
They'll outlast fancy lilacs
woody hydrangeas
ever-green hostas

which sometimes expire,
but never in-your-face
perfect pushy forget-me-nots.

Wandering in Weeds

Lilting branches declare blossoms to come
and right away I'm caught
scanning for favorites to protect
to free from invaders and anoint with breathing space--
minutes turn to hours, whole afternoons
of distraction and transportation
grabbing yanking discerning what to pull
edging around Asian lilies—most favored today
along with peonies, themselves outshining cone flowers
and rampant lilies of the valley that have spread unmercifully
right to the throats of each self-seeded young peony
which, if they all take hold,
will become a fragrant conflagration
of plush magenta perennials

like Opa said: *Give them breathing space*
and they give you back rewards.

I fall into motion, moving patch to patch,
wandering in weeds, grappling in dirt
troweling out dandelions
till I'm enveloped: planting watching shaping
a backyard escape into a different world

Good News Today: a house, a tree, and a jacket

Spread across the country, each in our own city,
we parents and our two sons got news
that landed like laurels of flowers
garlanded over my shoulders
even as the world shudders over his orange face . . .

First we learned our neighbors will spare the tree!
Then we discovered son Dave wore the birthday jacket I sent.
And the primo news, the really big event —
our son and his wife are buying a house!
a corner house with a garden
with the school across the street and Metro close by
(four-year old Max said there's a hill out back to roll down).

News item number two: our neighbors will spare the walnut tree
they'd threatened to cut down.
The big beautiful heroic expansive tree is saved—
a rare species, home to songbirds and nesters,
cardinals and chipmunks and crows,
a landmark tree that soars over our skyline
and hides the unwelcome new building out back.
We'll applaud this news as long as we live in our house,
likely as long as we live.

The third piece of good news seems minor but is major.

Dave wore the birthday jacket I sent him
on the day his friends celebrated his birthday.
That's two good news items:
He has friends in his new Seattle location *and* he wore the jacket.
(He called the jacket "worryingly hip"—which I take to mean he likes
    it.)

"Dance" to Elsewhere

Three artists – dancer, composer, filmmaker –
merged their arts into something
called simply DANCE, which became
the antidote to mounting TV scenes of catastrophe,
nuclear cylinders spewing steam,
cloaked and hooded, worried engineers.

A mesmerizing show of men and women
soaring non-stop with elegance and speed
transported us away. Twelve sleek dancers
in slim white tops and flared white pants
flew out of darkness across the wide stage.

In pairs and foursomes, singly and grouped,
shifting, merging, and diverging, they danced,
complex as algebra, athletic as Olympians.
Filmed images, above, behind, in front,
repeated the dance and multiplied the dancers
twirling and leaping us into another world.

Electronic music echoed,
surrounding the dancers in sound
that wrapped and powered the scene.

A threesome – Lucinda Childs pillar of dance,
composer Philip Glass, filmmaker Sol LeWitt –
transported us beyond the catastrophe in Japan.

136

A place of many arts that knows the elegance of dance
now again knows devastation and heartache.

Kudos to Dr. Seuss

Our high fives, Kiki's and mine, hit just right—
hand to hand, solid—the thwack of a smack
echoed her pride. She read by herself today.
that Smack! shaped her day and rejiggered mine.

While there're Brazil's mosquitoes
spreading horrors,
and Flint's lead-carrying water
poisoning young children

First-grader Kiki
read for the whole hour, today,
no distraction into drawing or games.
I got it. I can do it, she said.

The brilliant Dr. Seuss—catchy rhymes,
hard words and easy, Kiki plowed on undaunted,
with focus and heart and wide-eyed interest,
her smiley seven-year old, snaggle-tooth
beautiful face close to the page.
She was working, sounding out the words,
keeping on keeping on
till we came to the end of our mentoring hour.

Nothing, not all the hugs her friends give her
or her sparkly sweaters, fluffy skirts or excellent boots,
interests her like the books she read today.

She glowed with excitement.

Her hard work, her spirit,
a gift in the face of Flint and Brazil.
We picked the best books for next week
and high-fived a jolly farewell.

Surprise Gift

By default, by command, by choice—
it's unknown territory to do this self-isolate agenda
to stock the pantry and the fridge and the freezer
to take the only exercise we can . . . walks
on which we encounter few to none
the occasional youngster with a dog
or oldster with a friend and a dog
to skirt up onto the grass beside the walkway
or walk down the middle of the empty street
to wonder at those who plow straight ahead not skirting
to move up wider yet onto the snowy edges
to avoid droplets in case one of them sneezes

but the reward, there is a reward
despite the anxiety, the long wakeful hours fearing you've got it
the headache in the night—is that a symptom?
too many blankets is being hot, it's not having a fever,
is the cough scratchy? I know that's a symptom. Is it **it?**

These rampant biting fears shrink to think of the real,
of people gasping for breath, schools closed
stealing friends and teachers and education
from children of all ages

the closed colleges changing the lives of the undergraduates
whose parents may not let them enroll next fall
far from home to that college where I spent 40 years at work.

Will it live? What else will crumble?

These are the real, the inescapable horrors—
the unspeakable decisions forced in ICUs and ERs
and the imploding economy around the world
the rising death rate here and in crowded Delhi
refugee camps already unthinkable, now beyond despair

BUT the reprieve, there is a reprieve—every morning at 10 a.m.
there he is on Skype, our seven-year-old grandson Max
who we've never before connected with like this—every day—
now this gift, a thorough-going escape into connectedness—
he says "unhuh" when I say "should I read the next chapter"
quiet, matter-of-fact, just "unhuh"

As many chapters as he wants, I'm there!
as long as his interest and his home-schooling agenda allow
today he told us about Jingava—a tv series he likes
but he doesn't think grownups would like it—
it's fellows made of Legos, he said, who have adventures

he also told us what an idiom is and that he's playing chess online—
and did some square-roots that Opa asked him

a thorough-going escape from the news spreading around us—
the joy of Max—salvation for the rest of the day, until tomorrow.

Praise Max!

Revelations in Time

Limoncello Helps

We weren't all there. The phone rang.
She said she didn't know where she was.
We've aged, our members are fewer,
but we don't expect to get lost after all these years
on the way to one or another
of our familiar homes for our book club/food fest.

Yet that fear lurks in each of us:
to be lost, in the dark, driving alone.
After another failed attempt, she just went home.
But her husband said, 'you're going; I'm driving you.'
And he did and she did and she brought her dish,
excellent vegetables to balance our plates.

Each of us admitted and tried to make her believe
we'd been lost in the dark alone at night
getting to one or another of our meetings.
It was no disgrace; night driving looms harder.
Our houses are spread along Vermont roads
and none has street lights

We all knew it could have been us; it has been us.
It could have meant more.
It could have meant what we all deny.
It could have meant the dreaded diminishments to come
as we change, as our group shrinks, as our children have children
as we label each twinge the start of something bad

as we try to brush it off, ignore it, take long walks, drink green
    smoothies.
It could mean the undeniable, the inevitable.
We're none of us stupid.
Reality creeps in despite exercise and healthy food.

And so we ended the night with a wisp of Limoncello
Limoncello to cement our connection
to applaud our Italian host whose food is always the best
(with doses of cream and butter and cheese)!
Limoncello to go with the flourless chocolate cake that none could
    resist
Limoncello to toast our gathering—one more night together,
and another inscribed on the calendar ahead

Reality Intrudes

The trajectory took a sharp turn,
a new focus was thrust forward
almost by stealth. But inescapable.
It landed without exclamation
right there, and stayed, and resonates still.
We five friends at a restaurant table
weren't discussing concerts or musicians,
as we often did, or movies or children or grandchildren.
Instead there we were opining on
where to get the best audiology test,
how to turn on the subscript of words
even if the TV series is in English,
what to do about aching knees, tendinitis, uncertain balance,
skis left in the closet this year (and last),
what to do with a big house when we can't make the stairs
and what about the plague of stashed belongings:
party dresses, books, letters, photos, children's spiral-bound
          notebooks,
their toys, grade school report cards . . .

How did this happen, this conversation
proclaiming a reality we've fallen into unawares.
Now we're smack in it, bandying about surprising topics
which I hear, unprepared, yet not surprised, in fact, a participant.

Then the latent threat of the big quiet emerged,
potent for each of us long-married ladies.

She of recent loss spoke of the astonishing silence, every room silent
after the death of her spouse of fifty-four years.
Now she's using a blowtorch to defrost pipes by herself.
He's gone just six months,
and the legal medical financial brokers hover, wanting answers now.

We agreed without fanfare that night driving is mostly out
and discussed friends who've moved into which senior home
and which one has good care and good food
and which has neither and should be avoided
and where can you get rides, and when is hospice called . . .

I can't go there. We're not there.
In our seventh or eighth decade we're keeping on keeping on
while these topics creep in, insinuate themselves
in growing challenges to sight and hearing, energy and sleep,
with hints of the dreaded loss of memory
as the ladies' lunch, with all kindness, spoke some unwelcome truths.

The New Car

a great silver sedan, a hybrid
suited to a person of a certain age
engineered to the nth degree
hoping for a brainy owner to do right by it
fearing it's fallen into the wrong hands

I can't even get the door to lock itself
and what about the heat, the AC, the tilting steering wheel
the forward backward, up and down
back-supporting seat, power mirrors
tune-seeker, station changer, garage-door opener
blue tooth phone hook-up
and smart key, way too smart for me.

Lucky we aging southerners grew up in cars:
driving at thirteen, licensed at fourteen,
motoring that big Impala wagon to high school
hanging with teenagers at the Zesto for burgers
or pulled pork at Maurice's Piggy Park
chatting with car-hops on walkie talkies
sneaking road trips from Columbia
to Charlotte and Charleston.

We drivers of that era of backseat encounters
fuzzy dice on rear-view mirrors, fur-covered front seats,
consider driving our Junior Johnson heritage.

These may not, however, be the best hands
for this well-made, eco-friendly, aerodynamic, fin-less car
to have fallen into.
Maybe it should have been a gas-guzzler
of roaring engines and dual exhausts . . .
I'm no Cale Yarborough, but his kid was in my class.
Maybe I've got the right pedigree—fantasy NASCAR roots—
to claim the tank-like fuel-efficient Toyota Camry hybrid.

Cutlery, etc.

there's something about a great big troublesome dinner
where you use all your good stuff
put boards in the table
find a cloth pure white to cover it—
gather the parts, the silver, the crystal, the china
his family's huge European fish knives
soup spoons with heft of a server
weapon-like forks from pre-war German households—
all those times and lives stolen from families
as they fled to New York

put Portuguese folk figures all down the center
pull out the stuff a mother knew a bride should have—
salmon-pink gold-rimmed china, silver set complete
place salt dishes and fairy-sized spoons
use wine glasses so thin they're a bother

her things bespeak a southern housekeeping
that hasn't quite taken hold
in my kitchen eating and backyard dining—
but the sweet times of the ladies book club,
when I pull out the stops and lay a fine table

my mother would smile on her own good teaching—
brisket sparked with Hungarian paprika
honoring her richly rowdy Jewish roots
served to the brainy bookish warm-hearted ladies from
Haiti, Iran, Germany, Britain
Chicago and Buffalo Springfield.

A Gaggle of Mothers

drove and flew and bussed to join together for a week
in a beach-front house on Billy Shore Road, Ryder Cove, Islesboro,
    Maine
September 2017

once there we five found ourselves
orchestrated by the music of birds, water, sunlight
and conversation about life and art, youth and age
and always sons and daughters, grandsons and granddaughters—

the dance of the birds, the walks and the water, the sunrise and shifting
    gold sunset
brought us together, us friends for fifty years

our days steeped in these gifts took us out of time
onto this island with its amazing blue heron
elegant, delicate, an ingénue, maybe a ballerina
who adopted us or we him
found in shallow tide waters on long long legs, strong and still
long graceful neck curved now and again
for a bite of fish caught in strong thick beak
gulped so quick then still again
then a soaring flight on extended wing to a seaweed-draped rock

always cormorants, preening and watching
strong in wide-winged flight
yet fixed all day atop each one's personal ball-shaped buoy

we gazed and gazed over smooth wondrous in and out tides
revealing evermore varied rocks and stones and shells
and undulating seaweed of rust and gold, brown and orange

we traipsed over sands and gathered aged nuggets of time:
stones, striped and pink, green and translucent

some of us with walking sticks

then our own beautiful pair of loons
one, then a dive, then two surfaced a distance away
and back again sweeping around each other
compact duckish black bodies, white neck, black spots
a family, calling in lyric whispers and warbles, gathering in

a cove of oft-maligned seagulls, scavengers of the inlet
showed their own dance after great chatter and squawk—
lining a long boulder in excellent array, one by one by one,
suddenly quiet, bird by bird assembled along the rock
their exact congregation reflected in still water
breathing in and out, on the inlet shore

bird lessons till our gaggle of mothers rose up and settled down
with stories and hugs and calls and meals
all together doing our kitchen handiwork
each with talents, stews, salads, soups, leftovers turned tasty
bookish ladies renewing deep ties over conversation, poetry,
the occasional unwelcome dive into sorry politics
about our beautiful earth under hostile oligarch threat
but always the dives towards our young and our own aging selves

lessons from each to each
from waters and tides, sunsets and wild flowers
creeping vines, cedars and pines, birches and berries

thistles, mosses and ferns
from heron and loon, gulls and ducks, skittering sandpipers
and one heroic bald eagle atop our island retreat

we gaggle of friends, gaggle of ladies, forever a gaggle of mothers

I think I love that fat furry rabbit.

Startling brightness at 4 a.m. Not a good sign.
Motion detector lights, ominous by design
easily tripped, sometimes by the neighbor's cats
but never at this wicked cold, late hour.
So bright I couldn't ignore it. Practically daylight intensity.

On a night I was tossing about
dwelling on the truth of getting old in the cold.
January in Vermont.
Fruitless wondering interfering with sleep.
But I was slipping closer to oblivion—and then the lights.

I left the comforting nest of warmth, partner sound asleep,
and bravely (!), stepped a bare foot on the cold floor.
I peered out the back window—no persons, no sounds
no human footprint in the snow
just very bright light exposing the scrabbly winter backyard—

occupied by a fat furry rabbit, a mottled brownish grey fellow
chowing down on bird seed beneath the feeder.
Did he joust with the pole to shake out more?
He was into it, unperturbed, oblivious to the light
head down, focused, fast chomping, not leaving,
carrying on, staying put, unaware, unconcerned that
he'd tripped the lights, undone the dark night

brought on full daylight making him the centerpiece the star,
captured unafraid in the spotlight of the drama.

He changed the subject.
He was the subject—
such focus, purpose, intensity,
a sight to see, a round mound, a furry beast,
an object to behold

broadcasting a quit-whining, seize-the-day kind of message.

New Skis

Winter plows on,
Hammering, relentless.
Dinners, martinis, tortellinis
Give ballast
But today's blank white sky
Brings more snow.
February holds tight—
So we took a wild leap.

Who tries cross-country skiing at our age
After a thirty-year hiatus
From the long, thin slippery sliders.
We were seduced I surmise
By the new no-wax, high-tech designs,
Easy clip-in clip-out bindings, sleek boots
The mystique of finding peaceful moments
In deep woods, gliding on skis
With only squirrels, rabbits, perhaps a snowy owl
To interrupt the quiet.

So we got the gear.
Plunked down a credit card for two sets.
Had the bindings attached.
And took to the undulant golf course
On a sparkling snow-covered afternoon
Confident we remembered the moves.

Then came the fall.
No physical damage
But he couldn't get up
Without a lot of flailing
Which went deep down
To doubt, I fear.

Now. Will we get back up and on?
Will we venture out again
On the smoothly manufactured
Highly efficient, technically proficient skis?
Sticks standing tall in the entry way
Taunt with their presence,
Skis, poles, boots, bindings.
All of it waiting to help us past February
And deceive us into the notion of ever young.

Celebrate We Must

Without glitter or trees or menorahs
or sons and their families with us this year,
we shaped a party anyway. Because, we must.
A birthday party for husband and dear friend.
Excess and extravagance required.
An evening to defy single digits outside,
the missing key players,
and fears of another wretched tweet-storm.
Our guests arrived well bundled
from the country to our small city house,
traded their boots for felted handmade booties,
and warm spirits mounted up.

First, tasty bites of cheese, olives, hearty bread
and Proscecco to toast the birthday twosome, the New Year,
and to counter 2017's legacy of horrors.
Tall tapering candles shone forth.
Colorful handmade ceramic farm ladies
marched down the center of the table
carrying baskets of chickens and eggs
heralding the plenty to come.
Rarely used china and silver and crystal
sparkled on the black and gold cloth.

Butternut squash, carrots and ginger, spiced the soup.
Waters and wines flowed forth.
Then chicken with thyme and rosemary, lemon garlic onion—

all hot roasted into crispy good eating
along with slim green beans and brown rice.
The *piece de resistance, coup de grace*—
'World's Best Chocolate Cake' of famed chef Yotam Ottolenghi—
sent us into overload. The primo guest,
husband of near half a century, thought the cake well-named
as did the rest of us, though dear friend ate only half.

Our age, our frigid weather, our children's troubles,
the horrifying, alarming, fascist-leaning politics
of he who shall remain unnamed plague us.
We chose instead to join hands, take heart, embrace friends,
enjoy the riches of food and music, fiction and poetry,
and make a celebration of perseverance, of carrying on
with gratitude for good fortune and good friends—while we still can!

A Gesture in Pink

Rushing to class, shouldering a backpack
using a walking stick to trek through the snow and ice,
he stopped, brought a vitamin B
to me at my third-floor attic desk.

Preoccupied with lecture thoughts
laced with mounting doubts,
he made sure we both had a B
in the hope it delays diminishments.

Does he still have it, he wonders.
He loves helping students to love poems,
to love the way the words work,
to find magic, sustenance there.
He's not sure he still has the strength
to meet the new faces, to get to know each one.

I receive the small pink pill
like a communion wafer or sip of Sabbath wine
honoring our shared life,
our ever-lasting worries about our children,
our dependence, our reaching out
as we move forward in the face of doubt
with our tenuous, yet flinty hold, each to each.

What were we thinking?

Charlie and Lio roar about
chase each other, catch and reverse
rumble and ramble with gusto
land atop tables, window sills even
turn in mid-air, leap heights six times their measure
arrive unscathed, wherever, rolling and roiling.
Paws circle the other, upside down, a-kilter, yet graceful,
then they leap, halt, sit, lie down—
asleep—in a curled heap
head to toe or toe to toe, radiating elegance.

These kittens entertain save when they sniff a flower
that tips a vase, spills water, roils books and papers to the floor,
or when they tangle in the cord of a window shade
or slide on a tablecloth sending framed pictures
into a heap, topped by small cat feet . . .

Then they're shut in a room—to rethink their unthinking ways.
Yeah. Right.
But what were *we* thinking, getting kittens? At our age?

They bring crazy life into this senior household.
Litter mates. Soft, furry, pointed ears, fetching blue eyes.
A beautiful pair, purring their happy ways.
"Good brother cats," our son says with long-distance affection.

But they won't quit trying to sleep on my head.

Surely we'll arrive at some rapprochement.
They're only four months old. Only five hefty pounds each.
After kitten-hood, things will become sedate.
They'll be cerebral, philosophical, calm
like T. S. Elliot cats.
Plump. Devoted. Self-contained. Handsome.
Adoring. Adorable. Cats.
Of course.

Lessons Learned

the hiatus of a broken ankle
the undoing of the everyday, the night and the day
the indignity, the necessity, the reality—
bumping down the stairs seated, likewise up the stairs
don't leave the book, the eyeglasses, the sweater
up or down when needed down or up
no gardening, walking, galivanting
a different focus—
weight-bearing the operative word—getting there the goal

progress now two months later almost erases the path
the once-a-week shower, the crutches
the loss of control, opinion, will, caring about such
shoulders aching from bearing down askew on a too-tall walker
(I'm shorter than the standard walker user)

memories of mother-in-law Ulle AKA Ruth or Oma
always with a walker
did I know what that took
the arm muscles, the exhaustion, the shoulders
never a word from her about that
and sister Betty the world traveler
now even a walker is too much
since a stroke she only attempts the walker
when her PT fellow holds her up by the belt

me and the walker and the crutches together only a short while

the struggles of Ulle and Betty stick fast in mind
while I've given away the walker and the crutches—
gone with the PT guy to someone else in broken need
I've progressed to a cane to learn to avoid a limp
big surprise—a cane can poke—that's something invigorating
the unexpected poke—
poke a chair out of the way, a cat in the path, a bush that needs pruning,
an annoying person (of which there are none—
no visitors now during the unspeakable virus)

I learned the benefit/requirement of being a couch-potato
of him doing it all—meals, dishes, cats, the litter box
tending me—with shower, clothing, meds, ice pack
testament to us, but mostly to him—he did it all—
the meals, the cane, the pillows, exercise equipment
doing, getting, fetching, caring without complaint
Now out of the high-tech ski-boot, into the fabric ankle brace.

What have I learned? Is it only to persevere and exercise?
Or to know what Betty and Ulle have endured.
Relearn balance. Use the now weight-bearing broken, mended ankle.
Heel toe, heel toe, plant the cane the right way.
Appreciate the generosity, attention, concern of my husband of
        fifty years
offered again and again—you can call it good fortune, but mostly I call
        it love

Retirement Guide

Seize Bengali dance.
Shun Solomon Seal's brief blossoms,
fading fronds, lyric decline. Not that.
Embrace devil-may-care Indian dance.

Grasp the glitter and swirl,
rhythmic bare feet tapping and slapping,
skirts whirling, fingers aflutter,
hands flicking nuisance away.

Embrace her. Vanish with elegance.
Dance into new realms beyond
work-a-day strictures steeped
in paranoid undercurrent.

Time now to seize Bengali dance,
let go decades of place in that place.
Time now to twirl into new realms
of surprise and exotic adventure.

The Geese and the Gold Leaves

Sure signs.

Geese and gold leaves
proclaim the inescapable end of summer

light diminishing, days shortening, dark descending
flowers gone, fruits withered,

the seasons in lockstep marching onward
and my own decades slipping by almost unnoticed.

The seasonal honks of geese a tuneless harking call,
theirs alone, harsh, poignant, strange.

Brave, outstretched fliers have launched their flight south
on extended wing, full of fiber and sinew and grit.

One goose was alone, swerving, desperate.
I could hardly look; I feared he'd got loose,
come unhinged,
was doomed to stray to exhaustion.

Then a bold V of geese appeared, heading north,
then another smaller V, also heading north,
the wrong direction, but they persevered,

determined, it seemed, to gather in the lone flier.

High in the sky, the loner merged with the phalanx,
all swerved, tilted, regrouped to one strong honking expedition.

The V turned south toward their destination
their long, unthinkably long journey—

what glory, what family, with the solo goose pulled into their fold.

Their fine honkings like a discordant metronome
keep them in order, proclaim the shifting season,
as a flutter of gold leaves
dance down in an elegant death spiral,
twirling before me full of portentous signs
speaking the seasons of a life.

Sustenance

A companion showed up for the lonesome horse in the meadow,
an aging, mild-mannered donkey now tasting the grass,
slowly moving closer, then nose to nose, learning the comfort
      of touch—
not mother and child, but what friends they are!

How lovely, aspirational, to see their quiet connection—
occasional strolling or chasing, mostly nosing along,
rescued both—the beautiful aging mare solo for too long
the *en-route*-to-demise donkey now sustenance for the horse.

Lucky to find a pairing even an unlikely one.
Parent and child, naturally. Husband and wife.
Teacher and child, sometimes—

Teachers know acting up can have hidden causes—can be riotous
      or charming,
may be all-consuming—hunger, chips for breakfast, fights at home,
      neglect
or just being a kid. Teachers see stuff, know stuff, step in, embrace,
give building blocks, chess boards, paints, not reprimands or
      corner chairs.

And what pairings classmates can be, buddies
life-sustaining buddies, now undone, remote.

Kids like surprises, masks, outdoor games, movement, action,

masks might be kinda fun, Halloween-like—
we hope they're not fixated like us on the no-touch, no-breath,
        floating infection
the dreaded ubiquitous spreading virus—that sets us adrift

The overwhelming potent mystery—the vice grip.
There's no time table. No assurance that hugs are safe.
And who knows what the wretched thing looks like,
those suction cups on the surface, disgusting—the awful red parts
shown in lurid drawings and multi-magnified photos
in the paper, on tv, online, again and again, horrible careless germs,
        writ large,
stuff you can't see or feel or taste, swirling into you—bringing slippery
        symptoms

and we're just trying to connect and not infect
yearning for the remembered sweetness of companions.

Acknowledgements

With gratitude and appreciation to my encouraging readers: Betty Lou Bradshaw, Jackie Paskow, Lisa Hantman, Annemie Curlin, Jack Neuhauser, Richard Sugarman, Emily Weir, Betty Ustun, Major Jackson, Suzi Wizowaty, Greg Delanty, Will Marquess, and Mark Tarnacki.

* * *

For four years I published several poems in poetry journals. Thereafter I submitted and continued to submit poems to the Saint Michael's College literary publication, *Onion River Review* (not connected to Onion River Press).

Prior publications (listed in order of appearance in this book):

- "We have an encounter sometimes in the garden," published with the title "Getting Used to Loss" in the *Onion River Review* in 2010
- "Okay, so the Red Sox Let Us Down, 9-29-11," published in *The Hawaii Pacific Review*, 2011
- "Taste," published in the *Onion River Review*, 2016
- "The Catastrophe Gene," published in the *Onion River Review*, 2009
- "Orion's Hill," published in the *Onion River Review*, 2020

- "Sheesham & Lotus," posted on the wall of the Ripton (Vt.) Community Coffee House, 2020
- "Bread and Puppet," published in the *Midwest Quarterly,* 2012
- "Dave setting off," published in the *Onion River Review,* 2020
- "Vessels of Touch," published in the *Onion River Review,* 2011
- "Bits and Scraps of 'Littlehood'," published in *Onion River Review,* 2010
- "Borscht," published in *Onion River Review,* 2016
- "Mystery Hegemony," published in *Onion River Review,* 2020
- "That Hallowed Space," published with the title, "The British Museum," in the *Onion River Review,* 2008
- "'Dance' to Elsewhere,' published in *Grey Sparrow,* 2011
- "Cutlery, etc." published in *Bridges: Jewish Feminist Journal,* 2008
- "I think I love that fat furry rabbit." Published in *Onion River Review,* 2018

About the author

Photo by Jeff Clarke

Buff Lindau was born and raised in Columbia, South Carolina. She earned a bachelor's degree in English from Goucher College and a PhD in English from the University of South Carolina. Her dissertation in 1976, on feminism in the English Novel, was one of the first in women's studies. She worked at Saint Michael's College for 40 years retiring in 2014 after working first as an instructor in the English Department, then as Director of Public Relations and subsequently as Director of Marketing and Communications. The staff leadership award, given annually at Saint Michael's, is named for her. She and her husband Huck Gutman, live in Burlington, Vermont. They have two sons, a daughter-in-law, a soon-to-be daughter-in-law, and a grandson.

CPSIA information can be obtained
at www.ICGtesting.com
Printed in the USA
BVHW071911201220
595727BV00003B/13